The Grilled Cheese
SANDWICH

The Grilled Cheese SANDWICH

EBURY
PRESS

Contents

OUR RECIPES

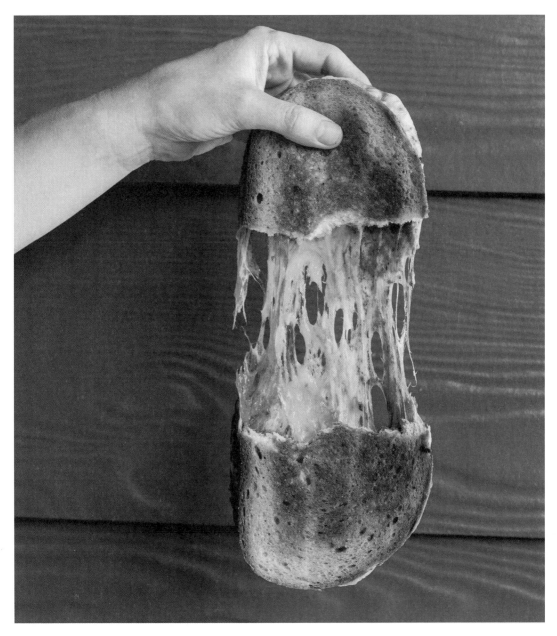

INTRODUCTION

Versions of the grilled cheese sandwich appear all over the world. It is a fantastic, cheap, quick meal or snack that can be eaten at any time of the day, mostly using ingredients you have hanging around in the fridge and cupboard – so what's not to love?

This book provides you with 60 recipes to inspire the grilled cheese lover in you. There are ideas for breakfast sandwiches, such as my California Dreaming, which includes goat's cheese, bacon and avocado. Fancy some lunch? How about the Grilled Cheese Club Sandwich? For dinner, perhaps something grown-up like my Rated R, which combines blue cheese and roast beef. If midnight munchies are what you're after, there are some naughty late-night feasts like the Return of the Mac, and even some dessert versions for those with a sweet tooth – Banoffee Toastie, anyone? Whatever cheese you like and whatever mood you are in, you will find a grilled cheese sandwich to satisfy your cravings.

Right, let's get started. There are various cooking methods for making a grilled cheese; I have listed them on the next page and given my thoughts on what works best. All you need to remember is that whichever method you choose, what you are looking to achieve is a crisp, golden exterior and melting, gooey interior.

PAN-FRYING/GRIDDLING

My preferred method, and the one that is used for the majority of recipes in this book. It's simple, you need very little equipment and, as you can see it cooking, it's easier to control.

SANDWICH/PANINI PRESS

This is my suggested method for recipes using ciabatta or focaccia as it manages to get the thicker bread crisp, but not burnt, whilst still melting the cheese inside. It is probably the quickest method to use as both sides are toasting at the same time.

GRILLING

You can make your grilled cheese by placing it under a grill – obviously! – but be careful as because you often can't see it, you don't have much control and it is easy to burn.

TOASTER

These days you can buy bags especially for cooking sandwiches in your toaster. This method is best used for sandwiches with less filling and nothing that is too wet or sloppy.

CAMPFIRE OR BBQ

If you are feeling adventurous you could try this – experiment with using a grill cage to keep your sandwich together or try a pie iron, which is a sort of press, that can go directly over the flames. You could also just place a frying pan on the barbecue or on a rack over a campfire. Temperature control will be quite difficult but outdoor cooking is always challenging so just be patient and give it a go - a campfire s'more toastie is a must!

As I mentioned, most of the recipes in this book are made using the pan-frying method but there are a few sandwiches for which I have recommended using a sandwich press. If you don't have a sandwich press, don't worry, you can still make these sandwiches. Just use the pan-frying method but weigh the sandwich down with something heavy, e.g. another pan with a few cans on top to create that pressure, and don't forget that you will still need to flip the sandwich to toast the other side. The methods I have used are suggestions but you can make the recipes with whatever equipment you have available to you. The list below gives you a guide to the basic equipment I would recommend.

RECOMMENDED EQUIPMENT

GOOD BREAD KNIFE – essential for getting your slices just the right thickness

SPATULA – for flipping and also to apply a little pressure to the sandwich as it cooks

BOX GRATER – to grate hard cheese, making it easier to distribute evenly

SHARP CHEF'S KNIFE – for slicing all the extra ingredients

MEASURING SPOONS – most measures in this book use spoons (they are level unless otherwise stated)

LARGE FRYING PAN – to give your sandwich plenty of space to create a crisp crust, and to make it easier for you to get under the sandwich with your spatula and flip

SCALES – for measures that can't be made using spoons

SANDWICH PRESS – totally optional, but if you love toasted sandwiches made using ciabatta or focaccia, or are extremely short on time, this may be worth investing in; they are pretty good value these days

You will notice that all the recipes in the book serve one, but they are easily doubled, tripled, quadrupled or more. If you can't fit all the sandwiches you want to make in the pan/grill/toaster at once just keep the made sandwiches in a low oven while you toast the rest. Next time you have your friends over, have a grilled cheese party – they will love it and it's so simple for you to do, not to mention cheap!

Now that we have discussed the best way to make a grilled cheese sandwich, we should talk a little about the types of ingredients used.

Firstly, and most importantly: the cheese! Below is a simple guide to types of cheeses that work well in a grilled cheese sandwich.

Some cheeses are much more suitable for grilled cheese sandwiches as they have better melting qualities. Cheeses with a high fat and high moisture content such as Mozzarella or Taleggio melt well at a relatively low temperature (around 55 degrees). Other cheeses that are much lower in moisture like Parmesan or Manchego melt at a much higher temperature (about 82 degrees) and will never produce that stringy melt associated with grilled cheese sandwiches. There are also some cheeses that are set using acid rather than rennet and because of this will never melt but rather just harden when heated as the moisture evaporates, these include fresh goat's cheese, ricotta and halloumi among others. It is worth keeping this in mind when making your sandwiches.

In the recipe introductions there are sometimes suggestions for cheeses that could be substituted should you not have the cheese called for. The general rule is that you can replace similar textured cheeses with one another, such as Gruyère for Comté or Camembert for Brie. Flavours may vary but the effect you are after will often be the same, so don't feel too restricted if you can't find one particular cheese; just follow this rule and pick another. Most blue cheeses are interchangeable with one another.

If you are after the classic oozing, stringy grilled cheese sandwich then the cheeses that do this particularly well are:

Mozzarella	Gouda	Emmental
Monterey Jack	Asiago	Raclette
	Taleggio	Muenster
Ogleshield	Provolone	Jarlsberg
Fontina	Gruyère	Cheddar
Havarti	Comté	

At other times you might choose a cheese not just for the melting qualities but also for flavour or suitability for the recipe. Other cheeses that can be used in these instances are:

Manchego	Reblochon	Mascarpone
Goat's cheese	Stilton	Ricotta
Parmesan	Roquefort	Labneh
Brie	Gorgonzola	Burrata
Camembert	Danish blue	Ossau-Iraty
Époisses	Cream cheese	Edam

There are so many varieties of cheese out there – more than I could possibly ever name – so this is just a loose guide; if you see an unfamiliar cheese or have a local cheese that you love, just give it a try.

In most of the recipes the cheese is grated to help it melt faster and more evenly, but note that when cheese is sliced in the recipes, such as the soft cheeses that cannot be grated, the slices are about 3–4 mm/⅛–⅙ inch thick.

The other essential ingredient in the grilled cheese sandwich is the bread. Breads that work best have quite a dense crumb and not too many large holes for the fillings to melt through. Sizes of bread vary so it is important to use the recipes as a guide, but also use common sense to adapt the amount of ingredients according to the size of your loaf. Here is a rough guide to breads that work well, but it is just to get you started; feel free to experiment.

TYPES OF BREAD

Sourdough	White farmhouse	Walnut bread
Wholemeal		Brioche
Rye	Fruit loaves, such as raisin bread or olive loaf	Challah/Milk bread
Ciabatta		
Focaccia		Multigrain
Crusty white bloomer		

Whilst we are on the subject of ingredients, it is always a good idea to think about things you could serve on the side to make it more interesting or substantial. It could be as simple as serving a pickle, fries, slaw or salad on the side, or maybe a scoop of ice cream with your sweet sandwich, even just using your favourite condiment to dip your sandwich in. A grilled cheese sandwich is also a great accompaniment to certain dishes, especially soups.

How about the four-cheese Somewhere Over the Rainbow dipped into a tomato soup, or a creamy celeriac soup with the Fontina Turner (fontina and salami) on the side? Perhaps a cup of butternut squash soup with the Spicy Chorizo Melt? The options are endless, so be creative.

Almost ready to start, but first here are my top tips to make the best grilled cheese sandwich possible.

- As you only use a few ingredients, make them the best you can afford.

- Cut your bread to a 1 cm/½ inch thickness for maximum crunch outside and gooeyness inside.

- When using butter in the recipes, always use room temperature butter for ease of spreading and even coverage.

- When possible, grate your cheeses for even distribution and a quicker melt.

- Moisture is the enemy of a crisp crust – be careful not to add ingredients with too much of them.

- Cook over a medium-low temperature so that you can ensure a crisp crust and melted centre.

- Brioche, challah and fruit loaf all brown faster as they have a higher butter and sugar content, so fry over a low heat for a shorter time, and keep an eye on them.

- If your sandwich is well coloured but the cheese hasn't quite melted, you can finish it by putting it in an oven at 200°C/Gas Mark 6 until the filling has melted. Be aware that not all cheese actually melts.

- Now you have all the tips and information you need, there's only one thing left to do … grill.

Chapter One

BREAKFAST AND BRUNCH

CALIFORNIA DREAMING

SERVES 1
PREP TIME 10 mins
COOK TIME 4–5 mins

This is a hearty start to the morning, full of good things. It is probably best saved for a weekend brunch when you have a little extra time to cook and digest.

INGREDIENTS

2 teaspoons olive oil

50g bacon lardons/cubed pancetta

1 tablespoon butter

2 slices brioche

1 tablespoon tomato chutney

5 slices goat's cheese

¼ avocado, sliced

1 egg

handful of rocket

Salt and freshly ground black pepper

TO SERVE (OPTIONAL)

Hot sauce

1 Place a large frying pan over a medium heat, add 1 teaspoon of the oil and fry the bacon lardons or pancetta until crisp and golden, then remove and set aside on kitchen paper to drain.

2 Meanwhile, butter both slices of brioche, using just enough to create a thin layer, then turn the slices over. Spread one slice with the tomato chutney and top with the goat's cheese, lardons or pancetta and avocado. Add salt and freshly ground pepper to taste.

3 Wipe the frying pan out with kitchen paper and place over a low heat. Carefully add the loaded slice of bread and the other slice next to it, butter side down. Fry for about 4–5 minutes until golden brown and crisp.

4 Meanwhile, add the remaining oil to a separate pan and fry the egg to your liking, seasoning to taste.

5 Carefully remove your open sandwich from the pan, top the loaded slice with the fried egg and rocket, place the other slice of bread on top and enjoy with a splash of hot sauce, if you fancy it.

MANCHEGO OVERBOARD

SERVES	1
PREP TIME	5 mins
COOK TIME	10–12 mins

Inspired by a Mexican quesadilla, this is a spicy kick-start to the morning. If you have any guacamole you could dip your toasted sandwich in it.

INGREDIENTS

3 tablespoons drained and rinsed tinned black beans

2 tablespoons drained and rinsed tinned sweetcorn

¼ avocado, diced

Small handful of coriander, chopped

3 heaped tablespoons grated Manchego

2 heaped tablespoons grated Monterey Jack

2 pickled jalapeño slices, drained and roughly chopped

1 tablespoon butter

2 slices sourdough

1½ tablespoons salsa

Salt and freshly ground black pepper

1 Mix the black beans, sweetcorn, avocado, coriander, cheese and jalapeño in a bowl. Season with salt and pepper.

2 Butter both slices of bread, then turn them over. Top one slice with the black bean and cheese mixture, spoon over the salsa and place the other slice of bread on top, butter side up.

3 Heat a large frying pan over a medium-low heat, add the sandwich to the pan and fry for 5–6 minutes each side, until it's a deep golden brown. Use a spatula to press down on the sandwich every now and then, to ensure the bread has good contact with the pan. Don't worry if some of the filling melts out in to the pan – it will be all crispy and taste delicious.

YOU DON'T KNOW JACK

SERVES 1
PREP TIME 5 mins
COOK TIME 5–6 mins

You can't go wrong with sausage and egg in the morning, and this sandwich uses chorizo to speed things up a little.

INGREDIENTS

12 cm/5 inch length of ciabatta

6 slices chorizo

1 teaspoon butter

2 eggs

4 heaped tablespoons grated Monterey Jack

Salt and freshly ground black pepper

1 Slice the ciabatta in half horizontally and top the bottom half with the chorizo; set aside. Heat a sandwich press.

2 In a small saucepan, melt the butter over a low heat. Meanwhile, crack the eggs into a small bowl, whisk with a fork to break up and season with salt and pepper. Once the butter is foaming, add the eggs. Allow a layer to firm up on the bottom before gently stirring with a wooden spoon until the egg is almost all set, then spoon it on top of the chorizo.

3 Sprinkle the cheese over the eggs, place the second piece of ciabatta on top and toast in the sandwich press for 5–6 minutes until the cheese has melted.

B.M.T.

SERVES   1
PREP TIME   10 mins
COOK TIME   5–7 mins

This is an Italian take on the classic B.L.T. You could use shop-bought or homemade pesto – whatever you have to hand.

INGREDIENTS

½ ball of mozzarella, sliced

3 rashers bacon

12 cm/5 inch length of ciabatta

1-2 tablespoons pesto

1 tomato, sliced

Handful of rocket

Salt and freshly ground black pepper

1   Place the sliced mozzarella on some kitchen paper to absorb excess moisture while you get on with preparing the rest of your sandwich.

2   Heat a large frying pan over a medium heat, add the bacon and fry for about 6 minutes until crisp on both sides, then place on a clean piece of kitchen paper to drain.

3   Heat a sandwich press. Cut the ciabatta in half horizontally and spread both cut sides with pesto. Add the mozzarella, bacon, sliced tomato and some salt and pepper to the bottom half of ciabatta, add the rocket and put the other ciabatta half on top.

4   Toast in the sandwich press for 5–7 minutes until the cheese is gooey and the bread is crisp.

PAN CON TOMATE

SERVES 1
PREP TIME 10 mins
COOK TIME 10 mins

In Spain this very well known dish I have based this sandwich on is made by rubbing garlic and tomato on grilled, olive-oil-saturated bread. You could swap the serrano ham for prosciutto or any other cured ham you have.

INGREDIENTS

2 slices sourdough

1½ tablespoons extra virgin olive oil

1 garlic clove, cut in half

1 large tomato, cut in half

30 g/1 oz piece of Parmesan

4 slices serrano ham

Salt and freshly ground black pepper

1   Put a frying pan over a medium heat. Brush both slices of bread on one side with half the olive oil and place, oiled side down, in the frying pan for 3–4 minutes until nicely coloured on the underside. Weighing them down with something heavy, such as another pan, will help them toast evenly.

2   Remove from the pan and rub the toasted sides with a half garlic clove and then half a tomato each, making sure you really squash the tomato in. Season with salt and pepper.

3   Using a vegetable peeler, shave the Parmesan into thin strips. Add the ham and Parmesan shavings to one slice of toasted bread, garlic- and tomato-rubbed side up, and top with the other slice, toasted and rubbed side facing down. Brush each side with the remaining olive oil and return to the frying pan for 3–4 minutes each side, applying pressure with your spatula to ensure an even colour.

CHERRY BABY

SERVES   1
PREP TIME   3 mins
COOK TIME   10–12 mins

Goat's cheese and cherries go together so well – if you haven't tried the combination before then give it a go, and if you have then you'll know what I'm talking about.

INGREDIENTS

1 tablespoon butter

2 slices walnut bread

1 tablespoon cherry jam

4 tablespoons crumbled soft goat's cheese

3–4 slices bresaola

1   Butter both slices of bread and turn them over. Spread one slice with the cherry jam then top with the goat's cheese and bresaola. Place the other slice of bread on top, butter side up.

2   Heat a large frying pan over a medium-low heat, add your sandwich and gently fry for 5–6 minutes each side, until golden brown.

GREECE IS THE WORD

SERVES 1
PREP TIME 2 mins
COOK TIME 10–12 mins

This breakfast is inspired by beautiful mornings in Greece, feasting on sun-ripened fruit and local honey. Labneh is a cheese made from strained Greek yogurt but if you can't find it, then goat's cheese would also work well.

INGREDIENTS

2 slices wholemeal bread

1 tablespoon butter

3-4 tablespoons labneh

2 fresh figs, sliced

3 toasted walnut halves, roughly chopped

2 teaspoons honey, plus extra to serve

1 Spread both slices of bread with butter and turn them over. Top one slice with the labneh, figs and walnuts and drizzle over the honey. Top with the other slice of bread, butter side up.

2 Heat a frying pan over a medium-low heat and place your sandwich in the pan. Fry for 5–6 minutes each side, until golden brown and crisp. Drizzle with extra honey to serve.

OM'ELETTE YOU FINISH

SERVES 1
PREP TIME 7 mins
COOK TIME 4–5 mins

Eggs are always a great start to the day: nutritious and filling. You can use your favourite soft herb here, or a combination of a few.

INGREDIENTS

2 eggs

1 teaspoon water

Small handful of soft herbs (such as dill, parsley, chives, chervil), leaves roughly chopped

1 tablespoon grated Parmesan

½ tablespoon butter

4 heaped tablespoons grated Comté

10 cm/4 inch length of ciabatta

Salt and freshly ground black pepper

TO SERVE (OPTIONAL)

Ketchup or hot sauce

1   Crack the eggs into a bowl, add a generous pinch each of salt and pepper, the water, chopped herbs and Parmesan, and whisk with a fork to combine. Cut the ciabatta in half horizontally.

2   Meanwhile, heat the ½ tablespoon butter in a small frying pan (about 15 cm/6 inch diameter) over a low heat until foaming, then add the egg mixture. Allow to cook until a layer forms on the bottom, then, using a palette knife, gently bring the cooked edges into the centre, allowing the uncooked egg to spread around the edges. Repeat this process until the omelette is almost cooked then top with two thirds of the Comté and use the spatula to fold each side in a third of the way across.

3   Slide the omelette onto the bottom ciabatta half and top with the remaining Comté then the other half of ciabatta. Heat a sandwich press and place the sandwich in and gently close. Allow to toast for about 4–5 minutes until the bread is crisp on both sides. Serve with ketchup or hot sauce on the side to dip into, if you like.

RICOTTA TRY THIS

SERVES   1
PREP TIME   15 mins
COOK TIME   8–10 mins

This sandwich tastes almost like a pie or tart, with creamy ricotta and sweet bursting blueberries. Any excuse to have a dessert for breakfast is a good idea in my book!

INGREDIENTS

40 g/1½ oz blueberries

1 tablespoon honey, plus extra to serve

3 tablespoons ricotta

Drop of vanilla extract

Finely grated zest of ½ lemon

½ tablespoon butter

2 slices brioche

Sprig of thyme, leaves stripped

1   Preheat the oven to 200°C/Gas Mark 6. Put the blueberries on a baking tray, drizzle with the honey and roast for 7–10 minutes until just bursting.

2   In a bowl, mix the ricotta, vanilla and lemon zest together, trying not to over-mix and loosen the mixture too much.

3   Spread the butter sparsely onto both slices of brioche and turn them over. Spread the ricotta mixture evenly over one slice, scatter over the roasted blueberries and the thyme leaves and place the other slice of brioche on top, butter side up.

4   Place a frying pan over a low heat, add the sandwich and cook gently for 4–5 minutes each side until golden brown. Serve drizzled with extra honey.

BORN IN THE USA

SERVES   1
PREP TIME   15 mins
COOK TIME   8–10 mins

The flavours of an American pancake breakfast in a toasted sandwich, this is for those who love that sweet and salty combination.

INGREDIENTS

3 rashers smoked streaky bacon

½ tablespoon butter

2 slices brioche

1 banana, mashed with a fork

3 tablespoons ricotta

Salt and freshly ground black pepper

TO SERVE

Maple syrup

1 Heat a large frying pan over a medium heat, add the bacon and fry until crisp on both sides, about 6 minutes in total, then place on a piece of kitchen paper to drain.

2 Butter both slices of brioche then turn them over. On one slice spread the mashed banana and season with a tiny pinch each of salt and pepper. Dot the ricotta over the banana, place the bacon on top and cover with the other slice of brioche, butter side up.

3 Wipe the frying pan out with kitchen paper and place back over a low heat. Add the sandwich and fry for 4–5 minutes each side until golden brown and crispy. Top with plenty of maple syrup to serve.

I BRIE-LIEVE IN A THING CALLED LOVE

SERVES	1
PREP TIME	20–25 mins
COOK TIME	10–12 mins

A dose of greens in the morning is always a great idea. You could make life even easier by roasting the greens the night before. Kale or cavolo nero would also work well.

INGREDIENTS

5 tenderstem broccoli stalks, trimmed

2 teaspoons olive oil

Pinch of chilli flakes, plus extra to serve

½ lemon

2 slices sourdough

1 tablespoon butter

½ tablespoon mayonnaise

⅛ red onion, very finely sliced

5 slices Brie

1 egg

Salt and freshly ground black pepper

1 Preheat the oven to 220°/Gas Mark 7. Place the broccoli on a baking sheet and toss with 1 teaspoon of the oil, the chilli flakes and some salt and pepper, and roast for 10–15 minutes until tender and slightly browned. Remove from the oven and add a small squeeze of lemon juice.

2 Spread both slices of bread with the butter and turn them over. Spread one slice with a thin smear of mayonnaise then add the charred broccoli, red onion and Brie and place the other slice on top, butter side up.

3 Place a frying pan over a medium-low heat and fry the sandwich, pressing down gently with the spatula every now and then, for 5–6 minutes each side, until the crust is a deep golden brown and the cheese has melted.

4 When you flip the sandwich add the remaining teaspoon of oil to the other side of the pan, crack in the egg, season and fry to your liking. Serve the sandwich topped with the fried egg and a few extra chilli flakes.

YOU'RE BACON ME HUNGRY

SERVES   1
PREP TIME   14–16 mins
COOK TIME   5–6 mins

This recipe uses familiar breakfast ingredients and turns them into a hearty breakfast grilled cheese sandwich that will keep you going all day long.

INGREDIENTS

2 teaspoons olive oil

3 slices prosciutto

2 field or portobello mushrooms, thickly sliced

2 sprigs of parsley, leaves roughly chopped

2 slices sourdough

1 tablespoon butter

1 teaspoon American mustard

5 heaped tablespoons grated Gruyère

1 egg

Salt and freshly ground black pepper

TO SERVE (OPTIONAL)

Hot sauce

1   Heat half the oil in a large frying pan over a medium heat, add the prosciutto and fry on both sides until crisp. Remove and set aside on kitchen paper to drain.

2   Add the sliced mushrooms to the same pan with a pinch each of salt and pepper and fry, stirring occasionally, until all the moisture has evaporated and they are lovely and golden. Add the parsley, stir and set aside with the prosciutto.

3   Spread both slices of bread with the butter then turn them over. Spread one slice with the mustard and top with the grated cheese. Place the mushrooms and prosciutto on the other.

4   Wipe the frying pan out with kitchen paper and place over a low heat. Add the topped slices of bread to the pan, side by side. Fry for 5–6 minutes until the bread is deep golden underneath and the cheese has melted. Carefully lift out of the pan onto a board.

5   Turn the heat up, add the rest of the oil to the pan and fry the egg to your liking, sprinkling with salt and pepper. Top the mushrooms and prosciutto with the fried egg and carefully flip the melted cheese side on top. Slice in half and let the egg ooze out. Serve with hot sauce on the side if you like it spicy.

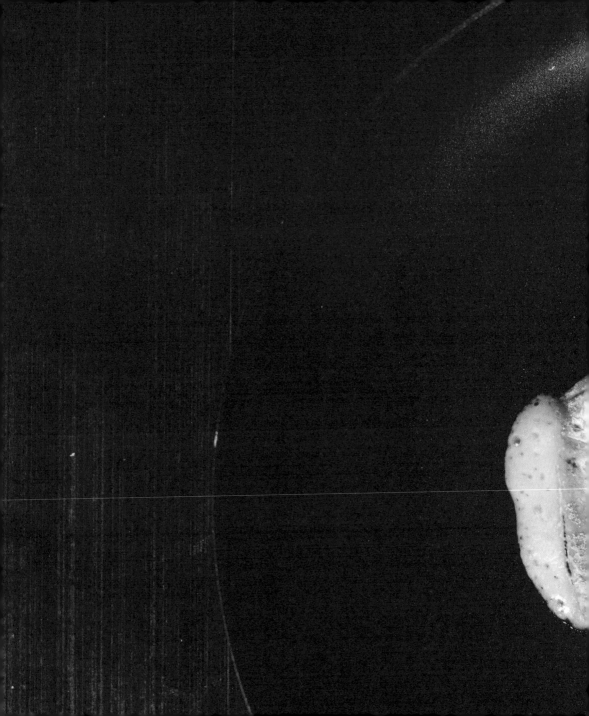

Chapter Two

LUNCHTIME
CLASSICS

DON'T BE A SAUERPUSS

SERVES 1
PREP TIME 5 mins
COOK TIME 10–12 mins

Sauerkraut, fermented cabbage from Eastern Europe with a sour flavour, pairs beautifully with the nutty cheese and dark treacly rye bread. This would be nice served with a little dollop of soured cream and chopped chives.

INGREDIENTS

½ tablespoon butter

2 thin slices seeded rye bread

1–2 teaspoons Dijon mustard

4 heaped tablespoons grated Gruyère

3 tablespoons sauerkraut

1 Butter both slices of bread and turn them over. Spread the mustard on both slices, top one with the cheese and the other with the sauerkraut and carefully sandwich together, buttered sides out.

2 Heat a frying pan over a medium-low heat, add the sandwich and fry for 5–6 minutes on each side until golden brown and the cheese has melted.

IN A PICKLE

SERVES 1
PREP TIME 5 mins
COOK TIME 10–12 mins

Toasted cheese sandwiches often have some kind of pickled element to cut through the richness, and this is a prime example of how that works so well.

INGREDIENTS

1 tablespoon butter

2 slices sourdough

1 tablespoon caramelised red onion chutney

2 heaped tablespoons grated Cheddar

2 heaped tablespoons grated Gouda

1 pickled onion, thinly sliced

TO SERVE

1 gherkin

1 Butter both slices of bread then turn them over. Spread one slice with the red onion chutney, top with both cheeses and then the pickled onion and place the other slice of bread on top, butter side up.

2 Heat a frying pan over a medium-low heat and add the sandwich, compressing it with a spatula. Fry for 5–6 minutes each side until golden brown and the cheese is oozing. Serve with a whole gherkin on the side for munching in between bites.

BETWEEN A ROQUEFORT AND A HARD PLACE

SERVES   1
PREP TIME   12 mins
COOK TIME   8–10 mins

The Roquefort works wonderfully with the sweet onion marmalade here, but you could substitute it with another of your favourite blue cheeses.

INGREDIENTS

Handful of kale

1 teaspoon extra virgin olive oil

½ tablespoon butter

2 slices brioche

1 tablespoon onion marmalade

30 g/1 oz Roquefort

Salt and freshly ground black pepper

1   Pull the leaves from the stems of the kale and finely shred. Put in a heatproof bowl, cover with boiling water and leave for 10 minutes, then drain and squeeze out any excess water then dab dry with a tea towel. Return to the bowl and toss with the olive oil and some salt and pepper.

2   Butter the brioche slices and turn them over. Spread the onion marmalade on one slice, pile on the kale and top evenly with the Roquefort. Place the second slice of brioche on top, butter side up.

3   Heat a frying pan over a medium-low heat and fry the sandwich for 4–5 minutes each side until it is golden and crisp and the cheese has melted.

POPEYE AND OLIVE

SERVES   1
PREP TIME   10–15 mins
COOK TIME   5–7 mins

Taleggio is a fantastic melting cheese from Italy, and here it coats the kale in a big gooey cloud. Havarti would also work, as would Asiago or Provolone.

INGREDIENTS

½ tablespoon olive oil

½ garlic clove, finely sliced

Pinch of chilli flakes

2 handfuls of kale, shredded

¼ lemon

12 cm/5 inch length of focaccia or ciabatta

1 tablespoon olive tapenade

5-6 slices Taleggio

Salt and freshly ground black pepper

1   Heat the oil in a frying pan, add the sliced garlic and chilli flakes and, as soon as the garlic begins to colour, add the kale and stir. Season, then add a splash of water, cover with a lid or foil and allow to steam for a few minutes until softened. Remove the lid or foil and fry the kale until all the moisture has evaporated and it is a little charred. Take off the heat and add a little squeeze of lemon juice.

2   Heat a sandwich press. Slice the focaccia or ciabatta in half horizontally, spread the bottom half with tapenade and top with the sautéed kale then the cheese. Place the other half of bread on top and toast in the sandwich press for 5–7 minutes, until it is crisp and the cheese has melted.

NEW YORK, NEW YORK

SERVES 1
PREP TIME 3 mins
COOK TIME 3–4 mins

A deli classic in toasted sandwich form. You could replace the Jarlsberg with Emmental or Swiss cheese.

INGREDIENTS

1 sesame or poppy seed bagel

½ teaspoon Dijon mustard

1 teaspoon mayonnaise

4–6 slices pastrami

1 small gherkin, thinly sliced

4 slices Jarlsberg

Salt and freshly ground black pepper

1 Slice the bagel in half horizontally. Combine the mustard and mayonnaise and spread on both sides. Top the bottom half with the pastrami, gherkin and cheese and season with salt and pepper. Add the top half of the bagel.

2 Heat a sandwich press and cook for 3–4 minutes until the cheese has melted.

COMTÉ OVER HERE, BABY

SERVES   1
PREP TIME   5 mins
COOK TIME   10–12 mins

The rosemary mayonnaise is lovely here but you could substitute the rosemary for basil, for a change.

INGREDIENTS

1 tablespoon mayonnaise

1 small sprig of rosemary, leaves stripped and finely chopped

½ teaspoon wholegrain mustard

1 tablespoon butter

2 slices rye bread

2 slices smoked turkey

½ avocado, sliced

4 heaped tablespoons grated Comté

Small handful of rocket

Salt and freshly ground black pepper

TO SERVE (OPTIONAL)

French fries

1   In a bowl, mix the mayonnaise, rosemary and mustard together and season with black pepper.

2   Butter both slices of bread then turn them over. Spread both slices with the mayonnaise mixture and top one with the turkey, avocado and cheese. Season and add the rocket then place the other slice of bread on top, butter side up.

3   Heat a frying pan over a medium-low heat and fry the sandwich for 5–6 minutes each side. Serve with French fries if you wish.

BEET IT

SERVES   1
PREP TIME   3 mins
COOK TIME   10–12 mins

This recipe is lovely with the beetroot chutney, but if you can't find it then caramelised onion chutney would work well too.

INGREDIENTS

1 tablespoon butter

2 slices walnut bread

1 tablespoon beetroot chutney

5 slices goat's cheese log

1-2 pickled beetroots, sliced

Small handful of rocket

Salt and freshly ground black pepper

1 Butter both slices of bread and turn them over. Spread one slice with the beetroot chutney and top with the goat's cheese and pickled beetroot, season with salt and pepper then add the rocket. Place the other slice of bread on top, butter side up.

2 Heat a frying pan over a medium-low heat and fry the sandwich for 5–6 minutes each side until golden brown and crisp.

AN APPLE A DAY

SERVES   1
PREP TIME   3 mins
COOK TIME   10–12 mins

Cheese and fruit is a wonderful combination and one that you will see more than once in this book. This particular one is based on the British ploughman's lunch that traditionally consists of cheese, pickle, bread and often an apple, among other things.

INGREDIENTS

1 tablespoon butter

2 slices walnut bread

1 tablespoon spiced apple chutney

4 heaped tablespoons grated strong Cheddar

½ crisp apple, thinly sliced

Salt and freshly ground black pepper

1   Butter both slices of bread and turn them over. Spread one slice with the chutney, top with the cheese and sliced apple then season with salt and pepper. Top with the second piece of bread, butter side up.

2   Heat a frying pan over a medium-low heat and fry the sandwich for 5–6 minutes each side until it is golden brown and the cheese has melted.

THE BIG CHEESY

SERVES 1
PREP TIME 3 mins
COOK TIME 5–7 mins

Loosely based on the flavours of the Southern American classic, the muffeleta, this is one for the meat lovers.

INGREDIENTS

Large pinch of smoked paprika

1 tablespoon mayonnaise

12 cm/5 inch length of olive focaccia or ciabatta

6 slices salami

3 slices mortadella or Parma ham

2 slices smoked ham

4 slices Provolone

1 roasted red pepper from a jar, torn into strips

Small handful of rocket

Salt and freshly ground black pepper

1 In a small bowl, mix the smoked paprika into the mayonnaise. Slice the bread in half horizontally and spread the mayonnaise mixture over both cut sides.

2 Top the bottom piece of bread with the salami, mortadella or Parma ham, smoked ham, cheese and red pepper, season with salt and pepper, add the rocket and top with the other piece of bread.

3 Heat a sandwich press and toast the sandwich for 5–7 minutes until the cheese has melted and the bread is crisp.

HEY P(R)ESTO!

SERVES   1
PREP TIME   10 mins
COOK TIME   5–7 mins

This is a great vegetarian option, both filling and super tasty. Comté or Gruyère would be good substitutes for the fontina.

INGREDIENTS

2 portobello mushrooms, stalks trimmed

Sprig of thyme, leaves stripped

1 tablespoon butter

10 cm/4 inch length of ciabatta

1 heaped tablespoon pesto

4 sun-dried tomatoes

3 heaped tablespoons grated fontina

Small handful of rocket

Salt and freshly ground black pepper

1 Preheat the grill to high. Place the mushrooms on a baking tray, season with salt and pepper, scatter over the thyme leaves and dot with the butter. Place under the grill for 6–8 minutes until cooked through.

2 Meanwhile, slice the ciabatta in half horizontally, spread the bottom half with the pesto and add the sun-dried tomatoes. Heat a sandwich press.

3 Once the mushrooms are cooked, transfer them to the pesto-spread ciabatta with all the lovely buttery juices. Top with the cheese and rocket, add the other ciabatta half and grill in the press for 5–7 minutes.

SERVES   1
PREP TIME   10 mins
COOK TIME   10–12 mins

INGREDIENTS

1 teaspoon olive oil

3 rashers smoked streaky bacon

3 slices white farmhouse bread

1 tablespoon butter

½ teaspoon wholegrain mustard

1 teaspoon mayonnaise

2 slices roast chicken or turkey

½ tomato, sliced

3 tablespoons grated Gouda

2 romaine lettuce leaves, stalk end trimmed

Salt and freshly ground black pepper

TO SERVE (OPTIONAL)

Potato chips

THE GRILLED CHEESE CLUB SANDWICH

An absolute American classic. Serve with potato chips for that authentic experience.

1   Heat the oil in a large frying pan over a medium heat and fry the bacon until crisp, about 3 minutes each side. Drain on a piece of kitchen paper.

2   Toast one slice of the bread. Spread the other 2 slices with the butter and turn them over. Mix the mustard and mayonnaise together and spread on both slices of bread.

3   Top one slice of bread with the chicken or turkey, tomato and cheese, and season with salt and pepper. Place the toasted slice on top and then the bacon and lettuce on top of this. Top with the final piece of bread, butter side up.

4   Wipe the frying pan out with kitchen paper and place over a medium-low heat. Carefully add the sandwich and fry for 5–6 minutes each side until golden brown then transfer to a board, slice into 4 triangles and serve with potato chips, if you like.

THE CLASSIC

SERVES   1
PREP TIME   3 mins
COOK TIME   10–12 mins

Who doesn't love a classic ham, cheese and tomato sandwich? The flavour is amped up here with the addition of tomato chutney.

INGREDIENTS

1 tablespoon butter

2 slices crusty white

1 tablespoon tomato chutney

2 slices honey-roast ham

4 heaped tablespoons grated strong Cheddar

1 tomato, sliced

Salt and freshly ground black pepper

1   Butter both slices of bread and turn them over. Spread one slice with the tomato chutney, top with the ham, cheese and then the sliced tomato. Season with salt and plenty of black pepper and top with the other slice of bread, butter side up.

2   Heat a frying pan over a medium-low heat and fry the sandwich for 5–6 minutes each side until it is golden and crisp and the cheese has melted. Use a spatula to press down on the sandwich every now and then to ensure good contact with the pan and a crisp crust.

Chapter Three

DINNERS TO IMPRESS

CAMEM-BURT REYNOLDS

SERVES   1
PREP TIME   3 mins
COOK TIME   10–12 mins

A great sandwich to use up all those Thanksgiving or Christmas leftovers. Brie also works well for those who prefer their cheese a little less pungent. If you use leftover turkey rather than pre-packed sliced, make sure it is thoroughly heated through.

INGREDIENTS

1 tablespoon butter

2 slices sourdough

1 heaped tablespoon
  cranberry jelly

3 slices turkey

5 slices Camembert

Small handful of
  watercress

Salt and freshly ground
  black pepper

1   Butter both slices of bread and turn them over. Spread one slice with the cranberry jelly then top with the turkey and cheese, and season to taste. Add the watercress and top with the other slice of bread, butter side up.

2   Heat a frying pan over a medium-low heat and fry the sandwich for 5–6 minutes each side until it is beautifully golden.

HONK IF YOU LOVE CHEESE

SERVES   1
PREP TIME   3 mins
COOK TIME   10–12 mins

Époisses is a wonderfully pungent soft cow's milk cheese that works really well with the sweetness of the quince paste. If you don't like Époisses you could use Brie, Camembert or Reblochon.

INGREDIENTS

1 tablespoon butter

2 slices walnut bread

1 tablespoon quince paste

4 slices speck or serrano ham

5 slices Époisses

Freshly ground black pepper

1   Butter both slices of bread and turn them over. Spread one slice with the quince paste, add the ham, then the cheese, season with pepper then add the other slice of bread, butter side up.

2   Heat a frying pan over a medium-low heat and fry the sandwich for 5–6 minutes on each side until golden brown.

UP TO NO GOUDA

SERVES	1
PREP TIME	8 mins
COOK TIME	10–12 mins

This is perfect post-Christmas when you have some cooked Brussels sprouts and plenty of cheese hanging around. You can substitute the sprouts for cabbage, kale or spring greens, and if you can't get bacon jam, use another favourite chutney.

INGREDIENTS

1 tablespoon olive oil

1 garlic clove, finely sliced

100 g /4 oz cooked Brussels sprouts, shredded

¼ lemon

2 slices sourdough

1 tablespoon butter

1 tablespoon bacon jam

3 heaped tablespoons grated smoked Gouda

Salt and freshly ground black pepper

1   Heat a frying pan over a medium heat, add the oil and garlic and fry until just beginning to brown, then pile in the shredded sprouts and season to taste. Sauté for 4–6 minutes until crisp and browned, then add a little squeeze of lemon juice.

2   Spread both slices of bread with butter and turn them over. Spread one slice with the bacon jam, pile on the sautéed sprouts and then the cheese. Season and top with the second slice of bread, butter side up.

3   Heat a frying pan over a medium-low heat and fry the sandwich for 5–6 minutes each side until it is beautifully golden and the cheese has melted.

RATED R

SERVES   1
PREP TIME   4 mins
COOK TIME   10–12 mins

Roast beef and blue cheese is a wonderful combination: deeply savoury and very grown-up.

INGREDIENTS

1 tablespoon butter

2 slices sourdough

1 teaspoon creamed horseradish

3-4 thin slices roast beef

4 tablespoons crumbled Stilton

Handful of watercress

1 tablespoon onion marmalade

Freshly ground black pepper

1   Spread both slices of bread with butter and turn them over. Spread one slice with a thin layer of creamed horseradish then place the slices of roast beef on top. Top with the cheese and watercress and season with pepper. Spread the second slice with the onion marmalade and place over the watercress, butter side up.

2   Heat a frying pan over a medium-low heat and fry the sandwich for 5–6 minutes each side until it is golden and crisp.

FONTINA TURNER

SERVES   1
PREP TIME   3 mins
COOK TIME   5–6 mins

An Italian spin on the classic ham and cheese: simple and delicious.

INGREDIENTS

12 cm/5 inch length of
ciabatta

1 heaped tablespoon
fig jam

6-8 slices fennel salami

5 heaped tablespoons
grated fontina

Handful of rocket

Salt and freshly ground
black pepper

1   Slice the ciabatta in half horizontally. Spread the bottom half with the fig jam then layer with the salami, cheese and rocket. Add salt and pepper to taste and place the other half of ciabatta on top.

2   Heat a sandwich press and grill the sandwich for 5–6 minutes until the cheese is oozing and the bread is crisp.

EXPAND YOUR CHORIZONS

SERVES	1
PREP TIME	10 mins
COOK TIME	5–6 mins

Evoking the flavours of Spain, this sandwich is a taste explosion.

INGREDIENTS

1 teaspoon oil

2 small cured chorizo sausages, split lengthways

1 teaspoon sweet hot paprika

1 tablespoon mayonnaise

12 cm/5 inch length of ciabatta

3 heaped tablespoons crumbled feta

1 shallot, very thinly sliced

1 roasted red pepper from a jar, torn into strips

Salt and freshly ground black pepper

1 Heat the oil in a frying pan over a medium heat, add the chorizo cut side down and fry until charred and crispy, about 4–5 minutes, then turn over and repeat.

2 Mix the paprika and mayonnaise together in a small bowl. Slice the ciabatta in half horizontally then spread the paprika mayo on the bottom slice. Top with the chorizo, feta, shallot and red pepper, season and add the top half of ciabatta.

3 Heat a sandwich press and toast the sandwich until the bread is crisp, about 5–6 minutes.

HEARD IT THROUGH THE GRAPEVINE

SERVES   1
PREP TIME   12 mins
COOK TIME   8–10 mins

The roasted grapes are great in this, but if you really don't have time you could always substitute them with a grape jelly.

INGREDIENTS

25 seedless red grapes

Sprig of thyme, leaves stripped

1 tablespoon olive oil

1 tablespoon butter

2 slices sourdough

5 tablespoons Gorgonzola

4 walnut halves, roughly chopped

1 tablespoon honey

Salt and freshly ground black pepper

1   Preheat the oven to 220°C/Gas Mark 7. Put the grapes on a baking tray, add the thyme leaves, oil and some salt and pepper and mix to coat. Roast in the oven for 10 minutes.

2   Butter both slices of bread and turn them over. Spread one slice with the Gorgonzola, top with the roasted grapes and walnuts and drizzle with the honey, then put the other slice of bread on top, butter side up.

3   Heat a frying pan over a medium-low heat and fry the sandwich for 4–5 minutes each side until golden brown.

THE MED

SERVES   1
PREP TIME   3 mins
COOK TIME   10–12 mins

This sandwich takes advantage of the fresh flavours of the Mediterranean. It also works well with pine nuts instead of flaked almonds.

INGREDIENTS

1 tablespoon butter

2 slices olive bread

1½ tablespoons good-quality pesto

5 tablespoons crumbled soft, rindless goat's cheese

1 tablespoon toasted flaked almonds

5 sun-dried tomatoes

Small handful of spinach

Salt and freshly ground black pepper

1 Butter both slices of bread and turn them over. Spread one slice with the pesto then add the crumbled goat's cheese. Top with the flaked almonds and sun-dried tomatoes, season with salt and pepper then add the spinach. Place the other slice of bread on top, butter side up.

2 Place a frying pan over a medium-low heat, add the sandwich and fry for 5–6 minutes each side until it is beautifully golden.

FEELING BLUE

SERVES 1
PREP TIME 8 mins
COOK TIME 10–12 mins

This is another great option for vegetarians. Feel free to use any favourite blue cheese instead of the Danish blue.

INGREDIENTS

2 portobello mushrooms

Sprig of thyme, leaves stripped

2 tablespoons butter

2 slices wholemeal bread

1 tablespoon onion marmalade

4 tablespoons crumbled Danish blue

1 tablespoon toasted pine nuts

Small handful of spinach, roughly chopped

Salt and freshly ground black pepper

1 Preheat the grill to high. Place the mushrooms on a baking tray, season with salt and pepper, scatter over the thyme leaves, dot with 1 tablespoon of the butter and place under the grill for 6–8 minutes, until cooked through.

2 Meanwhile, butter both slices of bread with the remaining butter and turn them over. Spread one slice with the onion marmalade, place the mushrooms on top, and scatter over the crumbled cheese then the pine nuts. Top with the spinach and then the other slice of bread, butter side up.

3 Heat a frying pan over a medium-low heat and fry the sandwich for 5–6 minutes until crisp and golden.

WANNA DATE

SERVES 1
PREP TIME 6–8 mins
COOK TIME 10–12 mins

Halloumi is a lovely, firm, salty cheese that works well with the sweetness of the dates. This is not your traditional grilled cheese sandwich, but give it a try – I promise you won't be disappointed.

INGREDIENTS

4 slices halloumi,
  1 cm/½ inch thick

1 tablespoon butter

2 slices sourdough

1 teaspoon harissa

4 Medjool dates, halved
  and stoned

Sprig of mint, leaves
  picked and roughly
  chopped

Sprig of parsley, leaves
  picked

1 Heat a frying pan or griddle pan over a medium-high heat, add the halloumi and fry for 2–3 minutes each side until nicely coloured.

2 Butter both slices of bread and turn them over. Spread one slice with the harissa and top with the halloumi, then the dates and herbs. Place the other slice of bread on top, butter side up.

3 Wipe the frying pan out with kitchen paper then return to a medium-low heat and fry the sandwich for 5–6 minutes each side, until it is a lovely, deep golden brown.

THE ITALIAN JOB

SERVES 1
PREP TIME 3 mins
COOK TIME 5–7 mins

A sophisticated toasted sandwich using primarily Italian ingredients. Use Provolone, Asiago or Havarti instead of Taleggio, if you can't find it.

INGREDIENTS

12 cm/5 inch length of focaccia

1 tablespoon wholegrain mustard

9 slices salami

4 artichoke hearts from a jar, thickly sliced

5 slices Taleggio

Small handful of spinach

Salt and freshly ground black pepper

1   Cut the focaccia in half horizontally and spread the bottom half with the mustard. Layer up the salami, artichokes, cheese and finally the spinach, season with salt and pepper and place the second half of ciabatta on top.

2   Heat a sandwich press and toast the sandwich for 5–7 minutes until the cheese has melted and the bread is crunchy.

STILTONY SOPRANO

SERVES 1
PREP TIME 3 mins
COOK TIME 10–12 mins

This sandwich is great for using leftover roasted, baked or mashed sweet potato or butternut squash – the sweetness works brilliantly with the salty blue cheese.

INGREDIENTS

1 tablespoon butter

2 slices wholemeal bread

65 g/2¼ oz roasted or mashed sweet potato

¼ small red onion, very thinly sliced

4 heaped tablespoons crumbled Stilton

6 pecans, roughly chopped

1 tablespoon honey

Salt and freshly ground black pepper

1 Butter both slices of bread and turn them over. Spread the sweet potato evenly over one slice, followed by the red onion, cheese and pecans, and season with salt and pepper. Drizzle with the honey and top with the other slice of bread, butter side up.

2 Heat a frying pan over a medium-low heat and fry the sandwich for 5–6 minutes each side, compressing it with a spatula every now and then, until it is golden brown and the cheese has melted.

Chapter Four

SOMETHING
SWEET

RAY LI-COTTA

SERVES 1
PREP TIME 2 mins
COOK TIME 6–8 mins

If you love chocolate orange then this one is for you. You could even have this for breakfast if the mood strikes.

INGREDIENTS

3 tablespoons ricotta

Finely grated zest of ½ orange

½ tablespoon butter

2 slices raisin bread

1 scant tablespoon marmalade

1 tablespoon chopped dark chocolate (or chocolate chips)

1 Put the ricotta in a bowl and mix in the orange zest. Butter both slices of bread and turn them over.

2 Spread the marmalade, then the ricotta mixture, over one slice of bread, and scatter over the chopped chocolate. Top with the other slice of bread, butter side up.

3 Heat a frying pan over a low heat and place the sandwich in the pan. Cook for 3–4 minutes each side until deep golden brown and the chocolate has melted.

BERRY NICE

SERVES 1
PREP TIME 2 mins
COOK TIME 6–8 mins

INGREDIENTS

½ tablespoon butter

2 slices brioche

2 tablespoons
mascarpone

Handful of mixed
summer berries

1 teaspoon honey

TO SERVE

Icing sugar

This is sort of like eating French toast: it's sweet, gooey and totally moreish. You could use raspberries, strawberries, blackberries or blueberries. Personally I like to use a combination of strawberries and raspberries.

1   Thinly butter both slices of brioche and turn them over. Spread one slice with the mascarpone, top with the berries and drizzle with the honey. Place the other slice of brioche on top, butter side up.

2   Heat a frying pan over a low heat, add the sandwich and cook for 3–4 minutes each side until beautifully golden, turning it carefully as this is quite a wet mixture.

3   Dust with icing sugar to serve. I would recommend a knife and fork for this one!

TO BRIE OR NOT TO BRIE

SERVES   1
PREP TIME   2 mins
COOK TIME   6–8 mins

If you have any leftover poached or roasted apricots lying around then they would be a wonderful replacement for the jam. You could also use another triple cream Brie if you can't find Brillat Savarin.

INGREDIENTS

½ tablespoon butter

2 slices brioche

1 tablespoon apricot jam

4 slices Brillat Savarin

1 tablespoon toasted flaked almonds

1   Butter both slices of brioche and turn them over. Spread one slice with apricot jam then top with the cheese and flaked almonds. Cover with the second slice of brioche, butter side up.

2   Place a frying pan over a low heat, add the sandwich and cook for 3–4 minutes each side until golden brown and oozy.

APPLE OF MY EYE

SERVES   1
PREP TIME   10 mins
COOK TIME   10–12 mins

This toastie is inspired by the warm aromas of apple pie, and would be great on an autumn evening, or morning for that matter (but perhaps without the cinnamon sugar). If you want to mix it up you could replace the apple with a pear.

INGREDIENTS

2 tablespoons butter

½ apple, cut into 8 slices

Pinch of ground cinnamon

1 tablespoon caster sugar

2 slices crusty white

2 tablespoons mascarpone

1 tablespoon roughly chopped toasted hazelnuts

TO SERVE (OPTIONAL)

Cinnamon sugar

1   Heat 1 tablespoon of the butter in a frying pan over a medium-high heat and, once foaming, add the apple slices, cinnamon and sugar. Toss to coat and allow to caramelise, turning occasionally, which should take about 3–4 minutes. Remove the pan from the heat.

2   Meanwhile, spread both slices of bread with the remaining butter and turn them over. Spread one slice with mascarpone then top with the caramelised apple slices and chopped hazelnuts. Place the second piece of bread on top, butter side up.

3   Heat a clean frying pan over a medium-low heat, add the sandwich and cook for 5–6 minutes on each side until beautifully golden, turning carefully so as not to lose the filling. If you have an extra-sweet tooth, then dust with cinnamon sugar to serve.

WHEN LIFE GIVES YOU LEMONS

SERVES 1
PREP TIME 3 mins
COOK TIME 6–8 mins

If you don't have any fresh blueberries you could substitute raspberries or, failing that, a generous tablespoon of blueberry jam.

INGREDIENTS

½ tablespoon butter

2 slices brioche or challah

2 tablespoons mascarpone

1 tablespoon lemon curd

Handful of blueberries

2 mint leaves, finely shredded

1 Butter both slices of brioche or challah and turn them over. Spread one slice with the mascarpone then lemon curd, and scatter with the blueberries and shredded mint. Place the other slice of brioche or challah on top, butter side up.

2 Place a frying pan over a low heat and cook the sandwich for 3–4 minutes each side until beautifully golden, taking care when turning it so as not to lose too much filling. Eat with a knife and fork!

GO BANANAS

SERVES 1
PREP TIME 3 mins
COOK TIME 8–10 mins

Bananas and Nutella are an absolutely classic flavour combination: you can't go wrong. Some toasted flaked almonds are a nice addition, should you want that added crunch.

INGREDIENTS

1 tablespoon butter

2 slices wholemeal bread

1 tablespoon cream cheese

1 tablespoon Nutella

1 small banana, sliced

Pinch of salt

1 Spread the butter on both slices of bread and turn them over. Spread one slice with the cream cheese, and the other with the Nutella. Top the Nutella with the sliced banana. Sprinkle with a tiny pinch of salt then place the other piece of bread on top, butter side up.

2 Heat a frying pan over a medium heat and cook the sandwich for 4–5 minutes each side until golden and crisp.

STRAW-BRIE

SERVES 1
PREP TIME 10 mins
COOK TIME 10–12 mins

The strawberries here are macerated, which sounds scary but it couldn't be simpler – it's just a process of sprinkling the berries with sugar, mixing and allowing them to sit. This draws the juices out of the fruit and it almost creates its own syrup. Once you try it you'll be doing it all the time.

INGREDIENTS

6 strawberries, thinly sliced

½ tablespoon caster sugar

1 tablespoon butter

2 slices white farmhouse

4 slices Brie

3 basil leaves, finely torn

Pinch of black pepper

TO SERVE

Icing sugar

1   Place the strawberries in a bowl, sprinkle over the sugar, mix and set aside for 10 minutes to macerate.

2   Butter both slices of bread and turn them over. Place the cheese on one slice of bread. Add the basil and pepper to the strawberries, stir to combine and pile on top of the Brie. Place the second piece of bread on top, butter side up.

3   Heat a frying pan over a medium-low heat, add the sandwich and cook for 5–6 minutes each side until the cheese has melted and the crust is golden brown. Dust with icing sugar to serve.

PEAR GRILLS

SERVES 1
PREP TIME 3 mins
COOK TIME 10–12 mins

This one is for those people who choose a cheeseboard over dessert. Nice and cheesy with only a hint of sweetness. If you have any dates, one or two halved would be a nice addition to this sandwich.

INGREDIENTS

1 tablespoon butter

2 slices walnut bread

4 tablespoons Gorgonzola

1 teaspoon honey, plus extra to serve

½ pear, thinly sliced

1   Spread the butter on both slices of bread and turn them over. Spread the Gorgonzola over one slice, drizzle with the honey and top with the sliced pear. Place the other slice of bread on top, butter side up.

2   Heat a frying pan over a medium-low heat, add the sandwich and cook for 5–6 minutes each side. Serve with an extra drizzle of honey.

ELVIS IS DEAD

SERVES 1
PREP TIME 2 mins
COOK TIME 10–12 mins

The sweet and salty combination of peanut butter and jam ticks all those craving boxes.

INGREDIENTS

1 tablespoon butter

2 slices sourdough

1 tablespoon crunchy peanut butter

1 tablespoon raspberry jam

1 tablespoon ricotta

1 Spread butter over both slices of bread and turn them over. Spread one slice with the peanut butter then the jam, and dot with nuggets of ricotta. Top with the other slice of bread, butter side up.

2 Heat a frying pan over a medium-low heat, add the sandwich and cook for 5–6 minutes each side until golden brown.

THAT'S JUST PEACHY

SERVES   1
PREP TIME   3 mins
COOK TIME   10–12 mins

One for a hot summer's day when the peaches are ripe and juicy. Serve with a scoop of vanilla ice cream to take this to the next level.

INGREDIENTS

1 tablespoon butter

2 slices fruit loaf

2 tablespoons cream cheese

½ peach, cut into 8 slices

½ tablespoon brown sugar

5 pecans, chopped

TO SERVE

Maple syrup

Vanilla ice cream (optional)

1   Butter both slices of fruit loaf and turn them over. Spread one slice with the cream cheese and add the sliced peach. Sprinkle with the sugar and pecans and place the other slice of bread on top, butter side up.

2   Heat a frying pan over a medium-low heat, add the sandwich and cook for 5–6 minutes each side until golden brown. Serve drizzled with maple syrup and, if you're really in the mood for a treat, a scoop of ice cream too!

BLACKBERRY CHEESECAKE

SERVES 1
PREP TIME 5 mins
COOK TIME 6–8 mins

This is essentially a cheesecake in toasted sandwich form. What are you waiting for?

INGREDIENTS

½ tablespoon butter

2 slices brioche

2 tablespoons cream cheese

Finely grated zest of ½ lemon

Drop of vanilla extract

Pinch of ground cinnamon

1 teaspoon honey, plus extra (optional) for serving

8–10 blackberries

½ tablespoon roughly chopped toasted hazelnuts

1 Butter both slices of brioche and turn them over. In a bowl, combine the cream cheese, lemon zest, vanilla, cinnamon and honey, then spread the mixture over one slice of brioche.

2 Scatter over the blackberries and hazelnuts and place the other slice of brioche on top, butter side up.

3 Heat a frying pan over a low heat, add the sandwich and cook for 3–4 minutes each side until golden and crisp. Serve with extra honey drizzled on top, if you like.

PLEASE SIR, CAN I HAVE S'MORE?

SERVES   1
PREP TIME   4 mins
COOK TIME   8–10 mins

An American campfire classic adapted to toasted sandwich format. If you are able, try making it on a campfire or barbecue.

INGREDIENTS

5 large marshmallows

1 tablespoon butter

2 slices white farmhouse bread

2 tablespoons mascarpone

2 scant tablespoons chopped dark chocolate (or chocolate chips)

1 digestive biscuit, crushed to rough crumbs

TO SERVE (OPTIONAL)

Chocolate sauce

1   Thread the marshmallows onto a metal skewer and toast over an open flame until they are charred and gooey.

2   Butter both slices of bread and turn them over. Spread one slice with the mascarpone then top with the chocolate, the toasted marshmallows and finally the crushed biscuit. Place the other slice of bread on top, butter side up.

3   Heat a frying pan over a medium-low heat, add the sandwich and cook for 4–5 minutes each side until everything is gooey and oozing. Leave to sit for a minute before eating. Top with chocolate sauce if you're feeling super-indulgent.

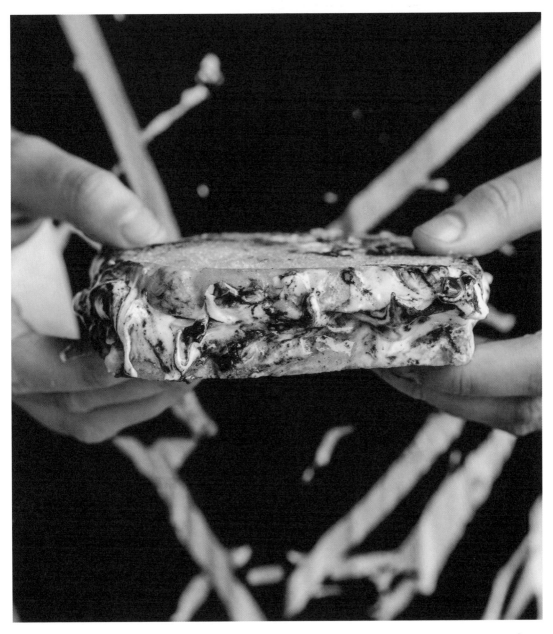

BANOFFEE TOASTIE

SERVES   1
PREP TIME   3 mins
COOK TIME   8–10 mins

Banoffee pie in a toasted sandwich …
ummm … yes please!

INGREDIENTS

½ tablespoon butter

2 slices sourdough

2 tablespoons
mascarpone

½ small banana, sliced

1 tablespoon dulce de
leche or tinned caramel

TO SERVE (OPTIONAL)

Ice cream

Extra dulce de leche or
caramel

1   Butter both slices of bread and turn them over. Spread one slice
with the mascarpone, place the slices of banana on top and drizzle
with the caramel. Add the second slice of bread, butter side up.

2   Heat a frying pan over a low heat and cook the sandwich for
4–5 minutes each side until golden brown and crisp on the outside.
If you are after ultimate indulgence, then serve with a scoop of your
favourite ice cream and extra caramel drizzled over the top.

CATCHER IN THE RYE

SERVES   1
PREP TIME   3 mins
COOK TIME   10–12 mins

Here's one for the slightly more adventurous diner; an unusual combination, perhaps, but totally delicious nonetheless.

INGREDIENTS

1 tablespoon butter

2 slices rye bread

1 banana, roughly mashed

3 tablespoons crumbled soft, mild goat's cheese

½ tablespoon honey, plus extra to serve

Salt and freshly ground black pepper

1 Butter both slices of bread and turn them over. Spread one slice with the mashed banana, season with a tiny pinch each of salt and pepper, add the crumbled goat's cheese and drizzle over the honey. Top with the other slice of bread, butter side up.

2 Heat a frying pan over a medium-low heat, add the sandwich and cook for 5–6 minutes each side until golden brown. Serve drizzled with extra honey.

Chapter Five

MIDNIGHT
MUNCHIES

SLOPPY JOE

SERVES   1
PREP TIME   8–10 mins
COOK TIME   4–5 mins

I've used leftover meatballs here but you could use anything similar that you have – a ragu or bolognese would be ideal, but even a chilli would work. This really is a feast!

INGREDIENTS

- 8 leftover mini meatballs in tomato sauce
- 15 cm/6 inch length of ciabatta
- 1 gherkin, thinly sliced
- 4 tablespoons grated fontina

1   Reheat the meatballs and sauce in a small saucepan until piping hot. Slice the ciabatta in half horizontally and spoon the hot meatballs and sauce onto the bottom half. Top with the gherkin and cheese then place the other ciabatta half on top.

2   Heat a sandwich press and toast the sandwich for 4–5 minutes until the cheese has melted. Be careful when eating, as this will be hot and messy!

THE ALMOST CUBAN

SERVES   1
PREP TIME   10 mins
COOK TIME   4–5 mins

INGREDIENTS

170 g/6 oz leftover BBQ pulled pork

15 cm/6 inch length of submarine roll or ciabatta

1 heaped teaspoon Dijon mustard

6-8 pickled jalapeño slices

40 g/1½ oz Swiss cheese, grated

Salt and freshly ground black pepper

TO SERVE

1 pickle

This is a simplified version of the meat-heavy sandwich known as The Cuban. If you have any other leftover slow-cooked meat, it would be a happy substitute here. Delicious served with a crunchy slaw, for freshness.

1   If your pulled pork is cold, place in a small saucepan with a splash of water and gently reheat until it is piping hot.

2   Cut the bread in half horizontally. Spread the bottom half with the mustard, top with the pulled pork, jalapeños and salt and pepper to taste. Add the cheese and place the other half of bread on top.

3   Heat a sandwich press and toast the sandwich for 4–5 minutes until hot through. Serve with a pickle on the side.

SPICY CHORIZO MELT

SERVES	1
PREP TIME	6 mins
COOK TIME	10–12 mins

Chorizo is a great standby to have in your fridge, as it keeps well and you'll be able to whip up this sandwich whenever you fancy!

INGREDIENTS

1 teaspoon oil

50 g/1¾ oz chorizo (about 1 small sausage), sliced in to 1 cm/½ inch chunks

1 spring onion, sliced

½ tomato, deseeded and diced

Small handful of coriander leaves, roughly chopped

4 heaped tablespoons grated Monterey Jack

1 tablespoon butter

2 large slices sourdough

Hot sauce

Salt and freshly ground black pepper

1   Add the oil to a frying pan and place over a medium-high heat. Add the chorizo and fry for about 3–4 minutes until crisp, turning occasionally, and adding the spring onion for the last minute of cooking, just to soften.

2   Meanwhile, mix the tomato, coriander and cheese in a bowl. Butter both slices of bread then turn them over. Add the cooked chorizo mixture to the cheese mixture with a pinch each of salt and pepper, and combine. Heap the mixture onto one slice of bread, shake over a little hot sauce and top with the other slice of bread, butter side up.

3   Wipe the frying pan out with kitchen paper and place over a medium-low heat. Add the sandwich and fry for 5–6 minutes each side until golden, crisp and melted. Serve with more hot sauce on the side.

THE KIM

SERVES   1
PREP TIME   2 mins
COOK TIME   10–12 mins

This one includes kimchi – a fermented spicy cabbage from Korea, where it is served with pretty much everything. A strong Cheddar is a great partner for its pungent flavour.

INGREDIENTS

1 tablespoon butter

2 slices sourdough

3 tablespoons kimchi

5 tablespoons grated strong Cheddar

1   Butter both slices of bread and turn them over. Add the kimchi and Cheddar and top with the second slice of bread, butter side up.

2   Heat a frying pan over a medium-low heat, add the sandwich and fry for 5–6 minutes each side until lovely and golden and the cheese has melted.

CHIP OFF THE OLD BLOCK

SERVES   1
PREP TIME   2 mins
COOK TIME   10–12 mins

Double carb heaven. Use oven chips here, or takeaway chips or fries to make things even easier. Alternatively, if you are really pushing the boat out, use your own homemade chips.

INGREDIENTS

1 tablespoon butter

2 slices white farmhouse bread

1 tablespoon mayonnaise, preferably in a squeezy bottle

1 tablespoon ketchup, plus extra to serve

1 large handful of hot, cooked chips

4 heaped tablespoons grated strong Cheddar

Salt

1   Butter both slices of bread and turn them over. Drizzle the mayonnaise onto one slice and then the ketchup, in a zig-zag fashion. Pile the chips on top, sprinkle with salt then add the cheese. Top with the other slice of bread, butter side up.

2   Heat a frying pan over a medium-low heat, add the sandwich and fry for 5–6 minutes each side until golden and the cheese has melted. Enjoy with extra ketchup for dipping.

WE'RE JAMMIN'

SERVES   1
PREP TIME   2 mins
COOK TIME   8–10 mins

If you haven't come across burrata yet, try and seek it out: it is creamy, gooey and delicious. If you can't find any, you can use mozzarella instead.

INGREDIENTS

1 tablespoon butter

2 slices fruit loaf

1 tablespoon fig jam

½ ball of burrata, torn

6 toasted hazelnuts, roughly chopped

1   Butter both slices of fruit loaf and turn them over. Spread one slice with the fig jam, top with the burrata and scatter over the hazelnuts. Top with the second slice of bread, butter side up.

2   Heat a frying pan over a medium-low heat, add the sandwich and fry for 4–5 minutes each side until the burrata is meltingly oozy and the bread golden.

RETURN OF THE MAC

SERVES   1
PREP TIME   3 mins
COOK TIME 10–12 mins

This feast is not for the faint hearted.
Total indulgence, but oh so worth it.

INGREDIENTS

1 tablespoon butter

2 slices sourdough

1 teaspoon Dijon
mustard

1 slice leftover mac 'n'
cheese, the size of the
bread you are using
and about 2 cm/¾ inch
thick

Pinch of cayenne

2 pickled jalapeños,
sliced

3 heaped tablespoons
grated Monterey Jack

1   Butter both slices of bread, turn them over and spread one slice
with the mustard. Slide the mac 'n' cheese onto the mustard and
top with the cayenne, jalapeños, cheese and, finally, the other slice
of bread, butter side up.

2   Heat a frying pan over a medium-low heat and fry the sandwich
for 5–6 minutes each side until the mac 'n' cheese is gooey and
hot through and the bread is golden and crisp.

MOZZAR-ELLA FITZGERALD

SERVES 1
PREP TIME 4 mins
COOK TIME 6–8 mins

This *mozzarella en carozza*, or fried mozzarella sandwich, could not be easier or more addictive.

INGREDIENTS

½ ball of mozzarella, thickly sliced

2 slices white farmhouse bread

1 tablespoon plain flour

1 egg

Splash of milk

2 tablespoons olive oil

Salt and freshly ground black pepper

TO SERVE

Chilli jam or tomato relish

1 Place the mozzarella slices on one slice of bread, leaving a 1 cm/ ½ inch clear border around the edge. Season with salt and pepper then place the other slice of bread on top and squeeze around the edges to seal.

2 Spread the flour on a plate and season generously with salt and pepper. Crack the egg into a shallow bowl, add the splash of milk and whisk with a fork to combine.

3 Heat the olive oil in a frying pan over a medium heat. Dredge the sandwich in the seasoned flour, making sure it is lightly covered, then dip into the egg to coat and place in the hot oil.

4 Fry for 3–4 minutes each side until golden brown, then remove from the pan to a piece of kitchen paper to absorb excess oil. This will be molten inside, so eat with caution.

SOMEWHERE OVER THE RAINBOW

SERVES   1
PREP TIME   5 mins
COOK TIME   10–12 mins

This is a fun one for kids to try, but us big kids will like it too. The Monterey Jack and mozzarella are here for their melting qualities, and the Cheddar and Gruyère for their flavour.

INGREDIENTS

1 tablespoon butter

2 slices sourdough

2 heaped tablespoons grated Monterey Jack

2 heaped tablespoons grated Cheddar

2 heaped tablespoons grated block mozzarella

2 heaped tablespoons grated Gruyère

4 different colours of food colouring (Recommended colours: blue, yellow, pink and purple)

1   Butter both slices of bread and turn them over. Mix the cheeses together and split equally among 4 bowls. Add a few drops of different colour food colouring to each bowl and mix to colour the cheeses.

2   Add the coloured cheese to the bread in 4 horizontal stripes, creating a rainbow effect. Top with the second slice of bread, butter side up.

3   Heat a frying pan over a medium-low heat, add the sandwich and fry for 5–6 minutes each side until the cheese has melted. For maximum visual effect, tear the toastie in half and gently pull apart to create a melted cheese rainbow!

THE 'I'LL HAVE WHAT SHE'S HAVING'

SERVES   1
PREP TIME   3 mins
COOK TIME   10–12 mins

Simple and satisfying: everything you want in a grilled cheese sandwich. If you don't have rye you could use wholemeal or even sourdough.

INGREDIENTS

1 tablespoon butter

2 slices rye bread

2 teaspoons American mustard

5–6 slices salt beef

1 pickle, thinly sliced, plus an extra whole pickle to serve

4 heaped tablespoons grated Swiss cheese

Salt and freshly ground black pepper

1　Butter both slices of bread and turn them over. Spread one slice with 1 teaspoon of the mustard and add the salt beef, sliced pickle and cheese, then another squeeze of mustard. Season to taste, then top with the second slice of bread, butter side up.

2　Heat a frying pan over a medium-low heat, add the sandwich and fry for 5–6 minutes each side until golden brown. Serve with the whole pickle on the side.

GLOSSARY

Brie — A soft cow's milk cheese with a white rind. Its flavours can range from mild to pungent depending on how mature it is. Brie melts well but into a pool rather than becoming stringy.

Brillat Savarin — A soft, white crusted cow's milk cheese that is so creamy and luscious it can be used in deserts. Its melting qualities resemble that of Brie.

Burrata — A young, fresh cheese made from mozzarella and cream. It has a mild, milky flavour and rich creamy texture and melts extremely well, becoming oozy and stringy.

Camembert — A soft, creamy cow's milk cheese with a pungent aroma and flavour, it melts well, becoming creamier but not stringy.

Cheddar — A hard, off-white cheese with a sharp flavour, it melts well and is a great choice for a grilled cheese sandwich.

Comté — A hard French cow's milk cheese with a rich, nutty flavour and fantastic melting qualities. Comté is ideal for grilled cheese sandwiches when you want the classic stretched cheese effect.

Cream cheese — Soft, creamy and mild tasting, this cheese is ideal for sweet grilled toasties. It holds its form surprisingly well when heated.

Danish blue — A semi-soft blue veined cheese that is sharp and salty. It is similar to Roquefort but with a milder flavour. Blue cheeses melt but not to a stringy consistency. Here, they are used for flavour.

Époisses — An extremely pungent smelling unpasturised cow's milk cheese, it's creamy in texture and salty and sweet in flavour. It melts into a creamy pool of cheesiness.

Feta — A firm pure white cheese from Greece, made either with sheep's milk or a combination of sheep and goat's milk, it has a distinctive tangy and salty flavour which is great although it won't really melt in your sandwich.

Fontina — A semi soft Italian cheese, it's rich, creamy, earthy and nutty and melts really well, an ideal choice for your toasted cheese sandwich.

Goat's cheese — The goat's milk used to make both the soft and rind varieties lends a tart flavour to this cheese. It also means that it does not really melt but just warms and softens.

Gorgonzola — Another blue cheese, this one is soft and buttery in its youth and crumbly and salty with a bit of bite from the blue veins as it matures. It works wonderfully with sweet fruity flavours.

Gouda — A yellow Dutch cheese, it has a mild, sweet almost caramel like flavour and melts beautifully-stringy perfection.

Gruyère – Sweet and salty and nutty but not overpowering, it is known for its superior melting qualities.

Halloumi – An unusual cheese that has a salty flavour and unique firm texture when cooked.

Jarlsberg – A mild cow's milk cheese with distinctive large holes, it's slightly nutty in flavour and is one of the best melters around.

Labneh – A soft, spreadable goat or sheep's yogurt cheese, a fantastic option for breakfast grilled sandwiches.

Manchego – A hard sheep's cheese from Spain with an inedible rind. It has a fruity, tangy flavour and is a great melter.

Mascarpone – A thick, creamy soft Italian cheese often used in desserts, this is perfect for all your sweet grilled cheese sandwich needs.

Monterey Jack – This cheese originated in America and is almost tailor-made for grilled cheeses due to its fantastic melting qualities. As it has a mild flavour it can be used in combination with another more strongly flavoured cheese to great effect.

Mozzarella – A fresh, milky, mild flavoured cheese, it is known for its unique stretchiness making it another perfect candidate for grilled cheese sandwiches.

Parmesan – As it only melts at high temperatures Parmesan is unlikely to melt in your sandwich but this cheese is all about delivering powerful savoury flavour.

Provolone – A semi-hard cheese with superior melting qualities and a good piquant flavour. It creates a lovely cheesy pillow when cooked.

Ricotta – An Italian whey cheese, it's creamy, white, fresh and slightly sweet making it another great option for your dessert sandwiches.

Roquefort – A moist sheep's milk cheese with blue veins that provide a unique tang and it is this that we use it for. It melts well but does not provide the stringiness associated with grilled cheese sandwiches.

Stilton – A semi–soft English cheese with a potent savoury and salty flavour and crumbly texture. It melts well.

Swiss cheese – This is a generic name for Swiss style cheeses with cartoon like holes made in America – they mostly resemble Emmental and are mild slightly nutty flavoured cheeses that melt well.

Taleggio – A semi soft Italian cheese with a strong aroma but relatively mild almost fruity flavour. It melts incredibly well, nice and oozy.

INDEX

10 9 8 7 6 5 4 3 2 1

Ebury Press, an imprint of Ebury Publishing
20 Vauxhall Bridge Road
London SW1V 2SA

Ebury Press is part of the Penguin Random House group of companies
whose addresses can be found at global.penguinrandomhouse.com

Penguin
Random House
UK

Text by Sian Henley © Ebury Press 2017
Photography © Haarala Hamilton 2017

Sian Henley has asserted her right to be identified as the author of this
Work in accordance with the Copyright, Designs and Patents Act 1988

First published by Ebury Press in 2017
www.penguin.co.uk

A CIP catalogue record for this book is available from the British Library

Commissioning editor: Grace Paul
Design: Wide Open Studio
Photography: Haarala Hamilton
Food stylist: Sian Henley
Props stylist: Georgina Low

ISBN 9781785035241

Colour origination by Rhapsody Ltd
Printed and bound in China by Toppan Leefung

FSC
www.fsc.org

MIX
Paper from
responsible sources
FSC® C018179

Penguin Random House is committed to a sustainable future for our
business, our readers and our planet. This book is made from Forest
Stewardship Council® certified paper.